PRIDE

by Deborah Crowdy
illustrated by Jodie McCallum

THE CHILD'S WORLD

Mankato, MN 56001

EVERYBODY says
I look just like my mother.
Everybody says
I'm the image of Aunt Bee.
Everybody says
My nose is like my father's.
But *I* want to look like *ME*!

—*Dorothy Aldis*

"Everybody Says" by Dorothy Aldis reprinted by permission of G. P. Putnam's Sons from HERE, THERE AND EVERYWHERE by Dorothy Aldis, copyright 1927, 1928, copyright renewed © 1955, 1956 by Dorothy Aldis.

Library of Congress Cataloging in Publication Data

Crowdy, Deborah, 1953-
 Pride / by Deborah Crowdy ; illustrated by Jodie McCallum.
  p. cm. — (Values to live by)
 Summary: Discusses justifiable pride and how it is manifested in daily life.
 ISBN 0-89565-566-7
 1. Self-respect—Juvenile literature. 2. Satisfaction—Juvenile literature. [1. Self-respect. 2. Conduct of life.] I. McCallum, Jodie, ill. II. Title. III. Series.
BF697.5.S46C76 1990
155.2—dc20
            89-48107
            CIP
            AC

When you have pride, you feel good
about yourself.

Pride is what you feel when you give
your mom the valentine you made for
her . . .

and what you feel when Grandpa
hangs your ornament right in front on
his Christmas tree.

Pride is what you feel when you
pledge allegiance to the flag.

And pride is what makes you walk
over to the trash can instead of
throwing your candy wrapper on the
ground.

When you have pride in yourself, you
take the time to do things right—like
smoothing out all the wrinkles when
you make your bed . . .

and making sure your hair is combed
and your clothes are neat and clean.

When you have pride, you don't give up on yourself—even when it seems you'll never learn how to ride your bike without training wheels.

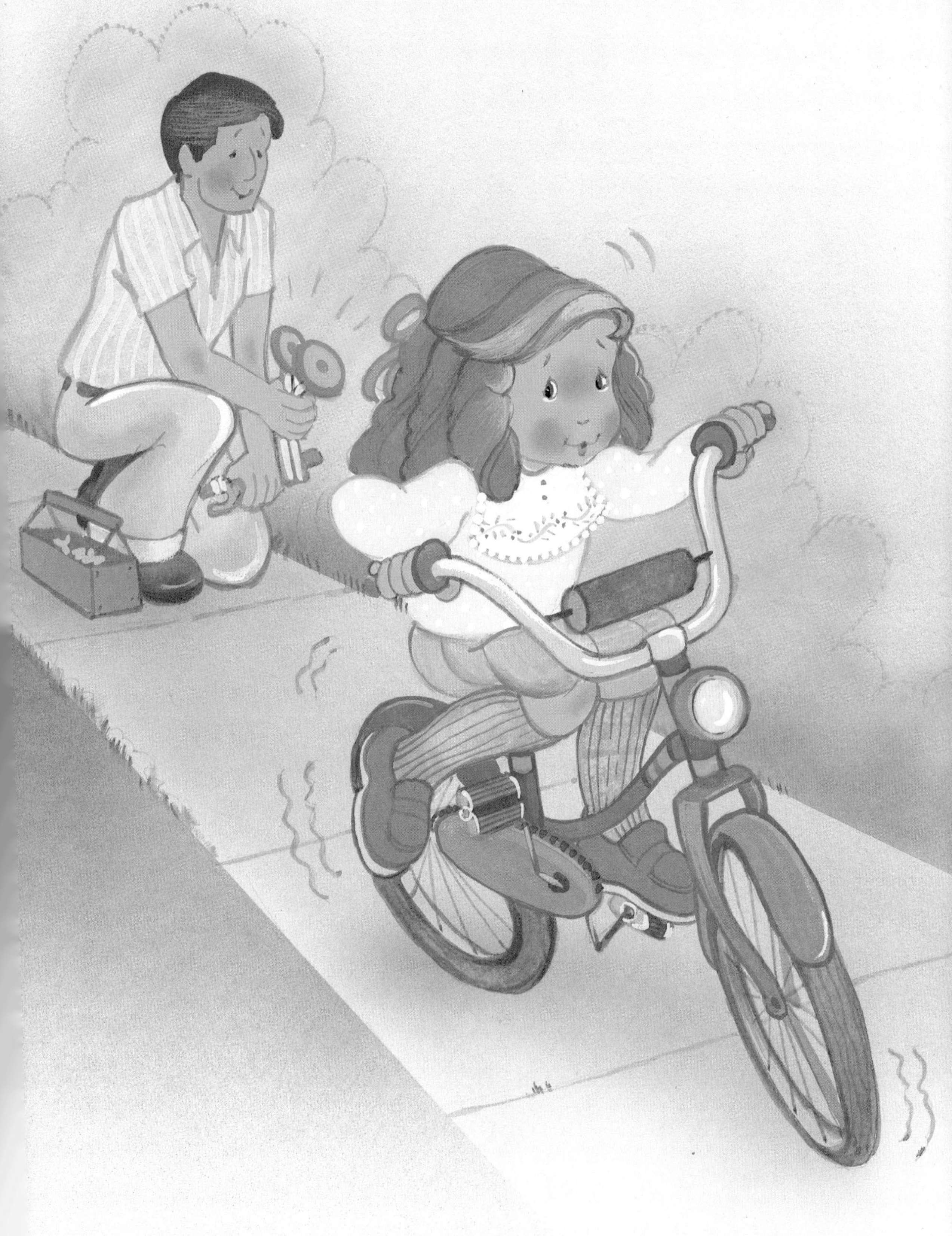

If you want to pitch, but the coach
puts you in the outfield, you'll do your
best to be a good fielder if you take
pride in yourself.

But bragging when your team wins the
game is not a sign of real pride.

You feel pride when you finally make
it . . .

all the way across the monkey bars.

And when you teach your little brother to count to ten, you really feel proud.

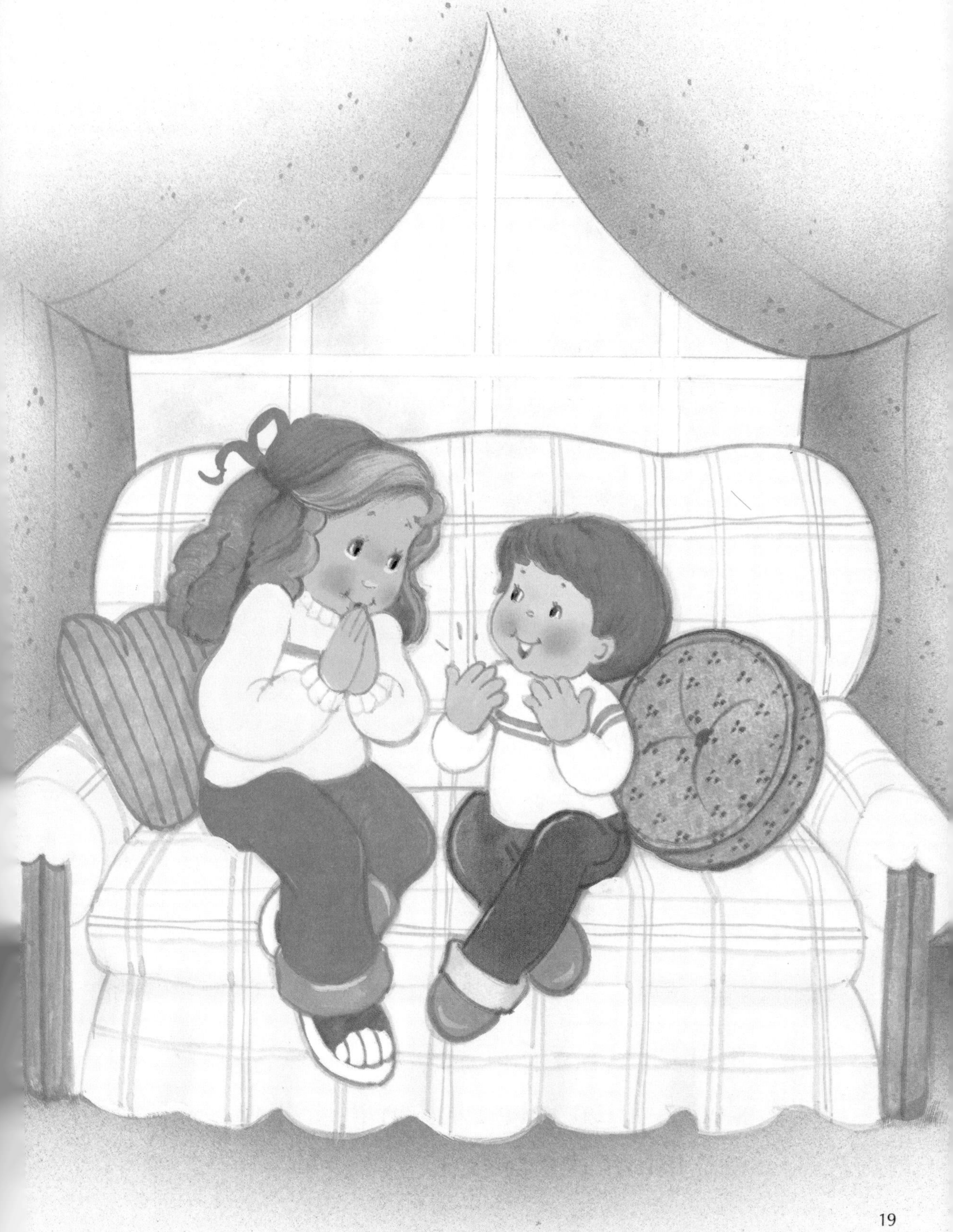

Pride is what makes you sure your
sled is great, even when it isn't the
newest or the fastest.

Pride is what you feel when your
teacher puts a smiley face on the story
you worked so hard writing.

And pride is what you feel when you have company for dinner and Mom trusts you with the special dessert.

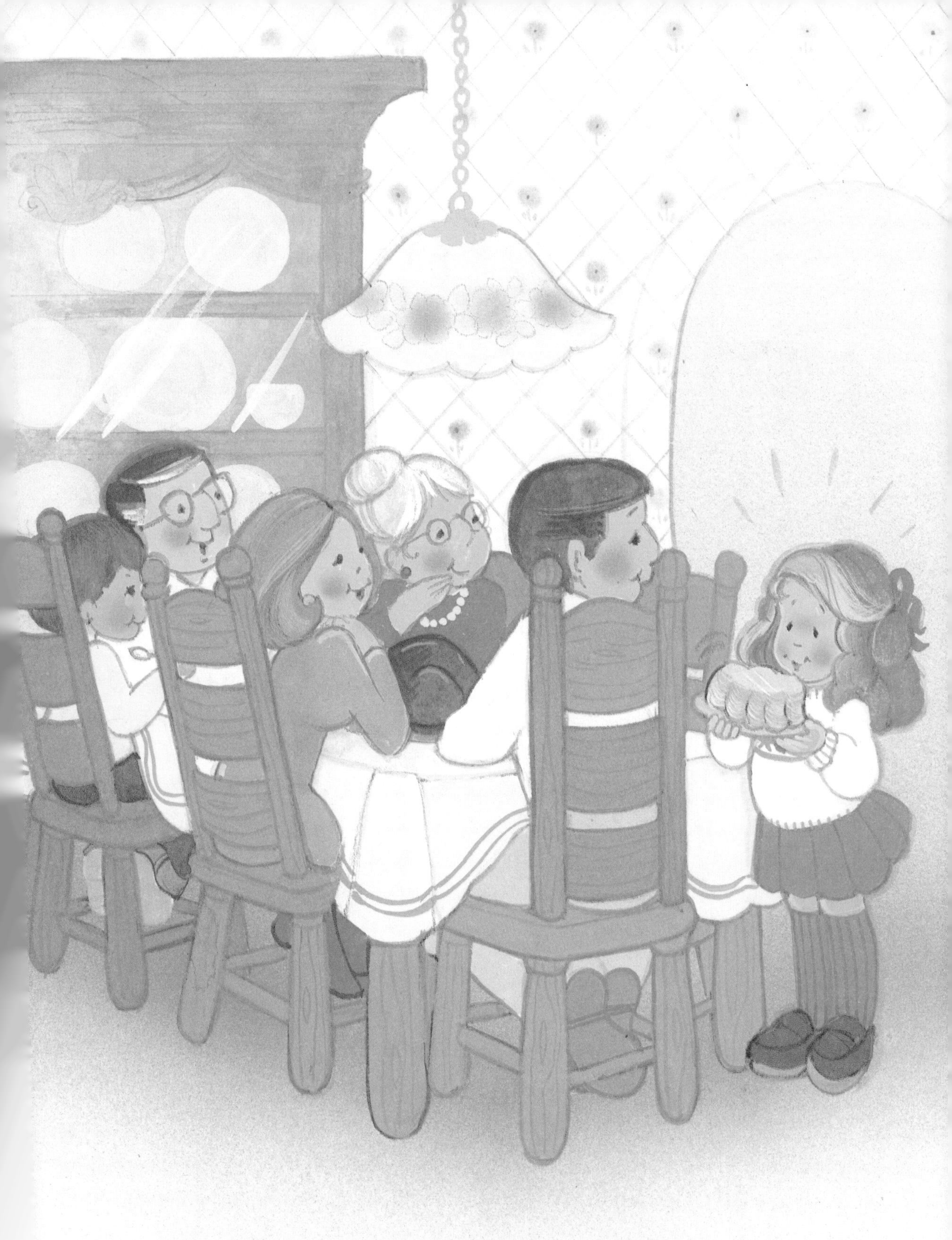

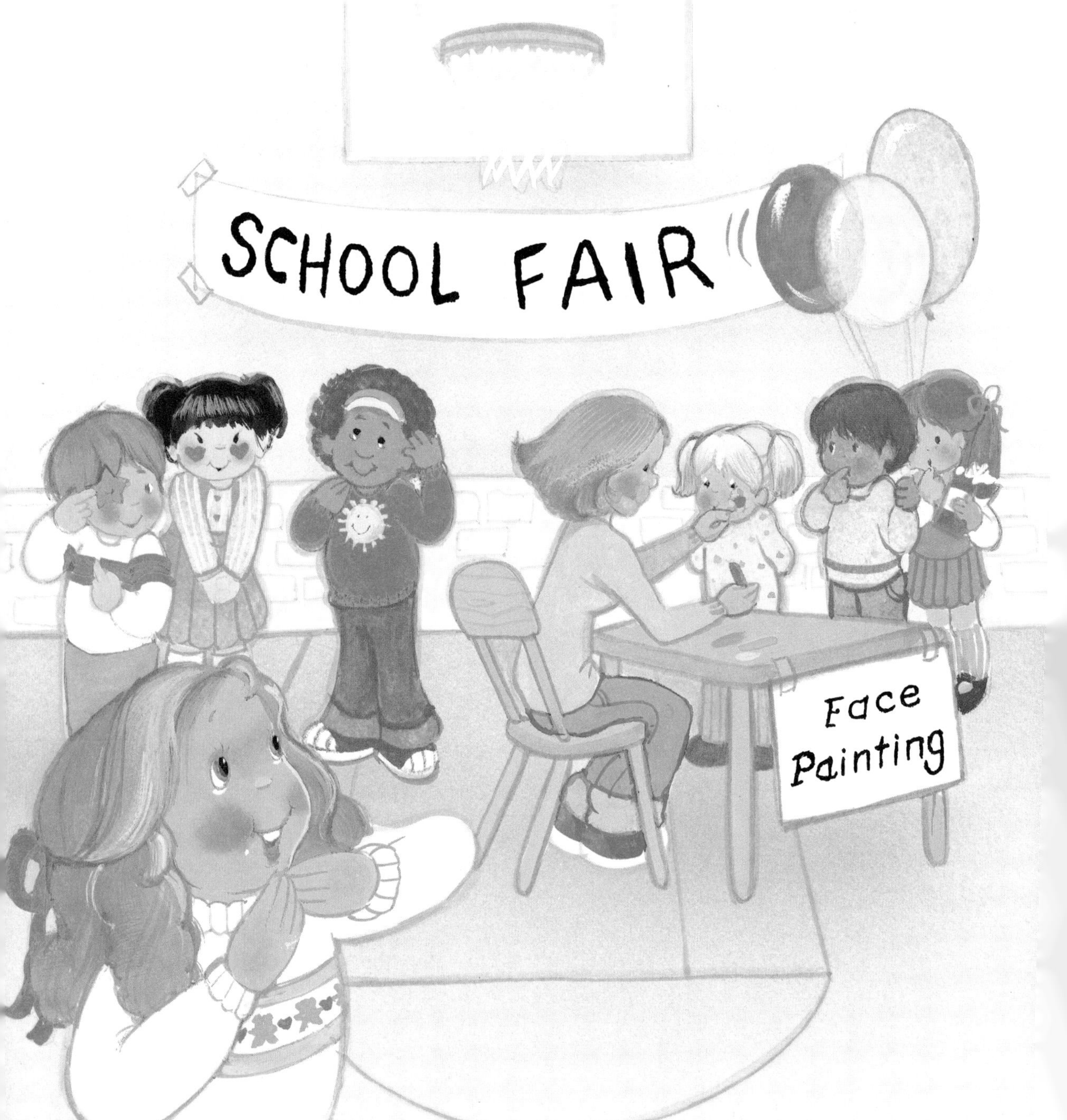
SCHOOL FAIR
Face Painting

When Mom helps out at the school carnival, you feel pride when you see all the kids whose faces she has painted.

And when Mom and Dad win a tug-of-war at the carnival, you burst with pride.

You feel a special pride when you know Mom and Dad are proud of *you*.

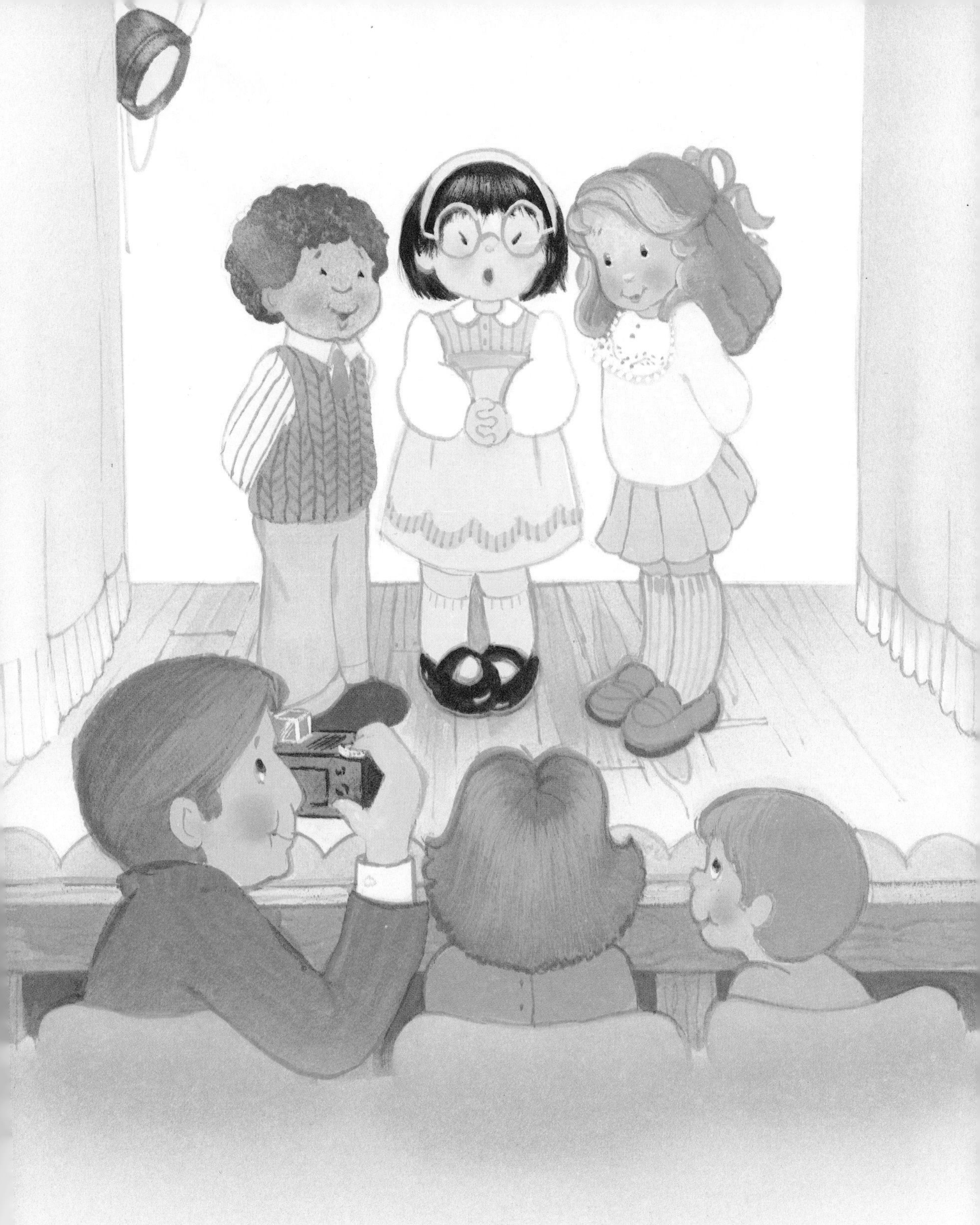

Pride is the feeling you have when
you win a race.

But even those who don't win can feel
pride when they try their best.

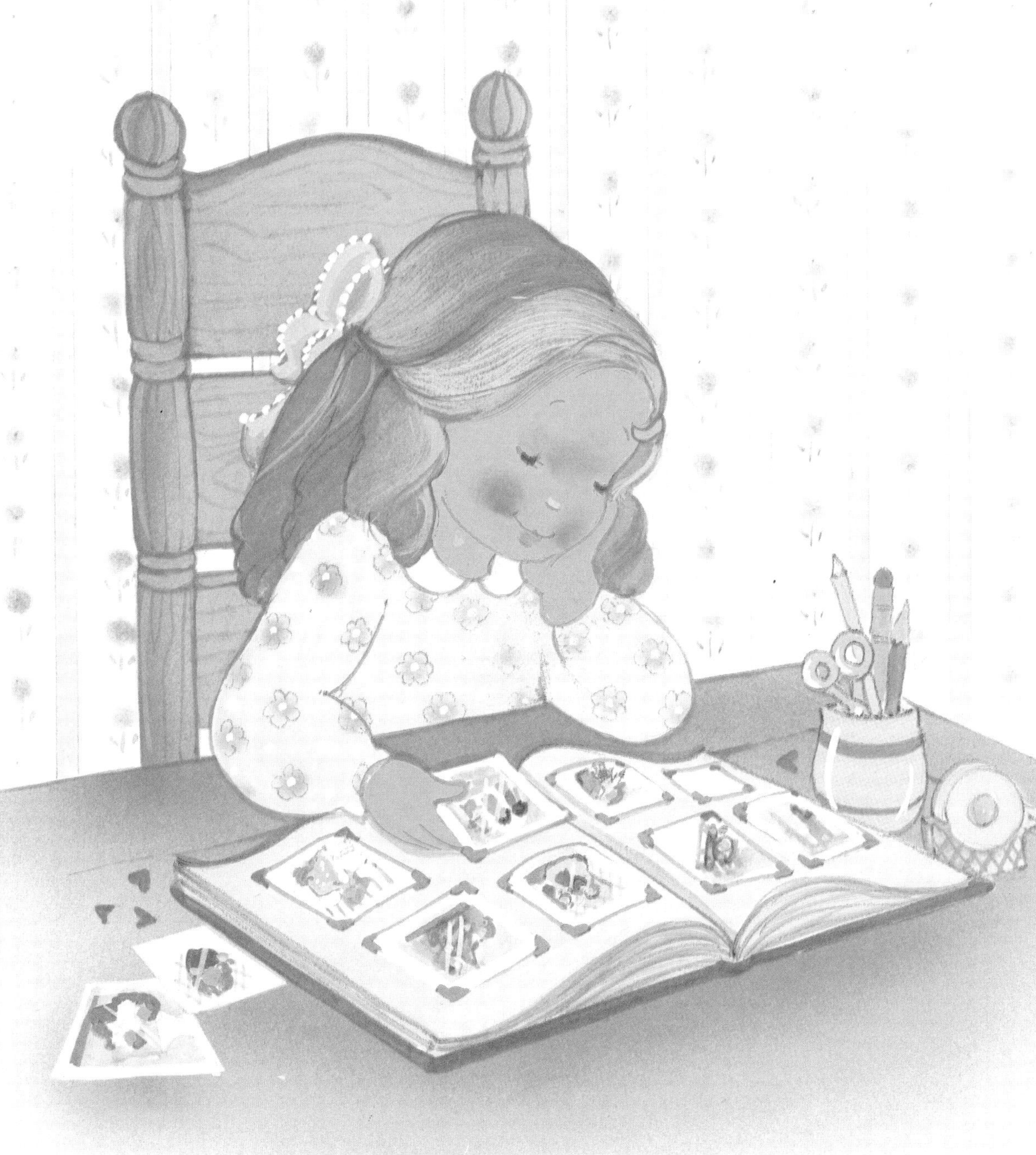

When you take pride in yourself, you know that there is no one else in the world quite like you—that you are special!